Power Through!

Specific Success Strategies
For Solopreneurs Who Want to
Change Your Destiny
One Day at a Time

Power Through!
Specific Success Strategies
For Solopreneurs Who Want to
Change Your Destiny
One Day at a Time

Printed in the United States

Dedication

This book is dedicated to you, my friend, if you've ever been told you won't amount to anything.

I reject the prediction and honor your magnificence!

Thank you to the precious people in my life...

To my father, Jean Wawa, and my mother, Songo Mabuku, who taught me to believe in God and in myself from a very young age.

To my wife Jacqueline, my children Tresor, Gabriel, Tanzey, Songo, and Eyenga, who encouraged me and provided motivation whenever my enthusiasm for engineering a book in a third language (English) faltered or fizzled.

To my friends Dr. Gail, Schoolfield, Mata, Vitale, and Kristine, who have engaged me in debate on the subject of fish tank thinking, sparking ideas or redirecting my thinking on a subject.

As a final thought, I know I have the ability to achieve goals I commit to pursuing. I demand of myself persistent, continuous action toward attaining them. Like you, I hope to leave a positive legacy at the end of life's journey. I sincerely hope that my efforts in bringing this book to you inspire you to make changes of your own so you, too, leave a lasting legacy that elevates and sustains your family and community for generations to come.

To success,

Dr. Matondo Gabriel Wawa

TABLE OF CONTENTS

Foreword

Pulverizing the Paradigm that Perpetuates Poverty

Dear Reader,

It should come as no surprise that you're an intensely intelligent individual. You're smart, talented, resourceful, and attuned to your community. So are many of the people in your community. So have you ever wondered why you continue to struggle when it comes to making ends meet and supporting your loved ones?

Here's why. You've been conditioned (by government and society) to expect less than you deserve—and far, far less than you're capable of achieving. You haven't been shown how to work smarter, not harder. (You work hard enough! It has been noted that if wealth were indisputably the result of hard work, most adults and lots of children would be multimillionaires several times over.)

WHAT ELEPHANTS, FLEAS AND FISH HAVE IN COMMON WITH HUMANS

ELEPHANTS

Hard-working Asian elephants in circuses (and elsewhere) begin life as calves that are staked to the ground while they're still too weak to uproot the metal stake that holds them in place. By the time they can easily uproot the stake, they've already "learned" (discerned) that freeing themselves is impossible. They have long since stopped trying to dislodge the stake and, as a result, they're forever bound by their limited understanding of their circumstances and of their exceptional abilities.

FLEAS

Fleas are immensely powerful insects: a flea can jump vertically up to 7 in (18 cm) and horizontally up to 13 in (33 cm), making the flea one of the best jumpers of all known animals (relative to body size)."

But here's the thing. Researchers discovered that by putting fleas into a 5" tall glass and covering it with a lid, the fleas quickly learned to jump no higher than 5"—even when the lid was removed! Once conditioned to a 5" ceiling, a flea "decides" it is forever bound by it!

FISH

Put a fish into a two-gallon bowl and it will grow to a certain size and stop. Put it into a ten-gallon tank and it will grow larger. Put it into a sizeable pond, lake or the sea and it will grow to the limits of its genetically-pre-programmed DNA!

Are you seeing a pattern here?

YOU

You live in a chronically-underprivileged community with poverty as your constant unwelcome sidekick. This has always been so, has it not? So you've been conditioned to expect no more. Perhaps it's simply easier to expect nothing more and get it than it is to expect more and risk being disappointed.

But here's the thing: You aren't an elephant, a flea or a fish. Your superior intellect and dauntless spirit tell you 'More is available!'

You know, to the core of your being, that a way over, under, around or through to a better future exists, if only you can find the path that will take you there.

And you're right: a better, brighter future does exist.

This guidebook has been carefully designed to point the way. So let's get going!

To your success,

Dr. Matondo Gabriel Wawa

CHAPTER ONE

Overcoming Victim Mentality Syndrome

"Whether you think you can or think you can't, you're right." - Henry Ford

Step One will be hard.

Step One will be making the decision to stop judging or blaming yourself and others.

It's going to be hard because we judge people all the time—if not consciously, then unconsciously.

Brains are pre-programmed for self-protection and survival. Discernment (judgment) is an imperative part of the equation whether you're a lizard, a leopard or a leader—and you're completely capable of being a great leader, so get used to the idea right now if you aren't already: it's part of the path to your success!

The amygdala—the part of your brain that emits dire warnings whenever you're in new territory or outside your comfort zone—judges whether it's safe to proceed or safer to just wait and watch.

As the resident of an underprivileged community, you've been conditioned to wait and watch—perhaps for an international aid truck—because up until now, not much else has offered sufficient hope to shift you into another gear. It takes relentless energy to break out of your circumstances, and when you're hungry, energy isn't easy to come by.

Victim mentality is a learned personality trait. It is acquired, not built in. Those who acquire it consider themselves victims of the negative beliefs and actions of others, and they think, speak and act in accordance with the belief.

You developed your present mindset while you were very young. You learned to limit your sights and goals as a direct result of family and community influences.

As an adult, it's quite likely that you often experience negative emotional states (anger, sadness, fear). You may blame others for situations over which you exercised some degree of control, too. You may be unwilling to take responsibility for your part in less than satisfactory outcomes. You might be a little paranoid (thinking others are out to get you, or evil) or envious (thinking others are just somehow luckier or happier by default). You may gossip to gain short-term pleasure and sympathy by telling tales of people who have aggrieved or aggravated you in some way. You may even have developed convincing arguments for why you're an unwilling fly caught in amber when it comes to your pitiful circumstances.

Victim mentality syndrome can cause negativity, self-absorption, defensiveness, the tendency to divide people into "good" and "bad", sloth, a feeling of helplessness, stubbornness, and self-abasement ("I'm no good. I'm just hopeless as a human being.")

If you find yourself saying things to yourself or others like "I can't..." "I must (do this because I have no other choice in the matter)" or "I don't know..." you're probably suffering from victim mentality.

But again: **Victim mentality is a learned behavior. You can** *unlearn it!* For example, let's say I'm considering getting a mortgage. I'm aware that the Reserve Bank may raise interest rates and that my bank will pass the increase on to me which will increase my monthly payments. I have no direct control over the Reserve Bank or what my bank will do.

But I can control my risk by choosing a fixed or variable rate mortgage. I can increase or decrease my monthly payments (within reason). I can increase the frequency of my payments. So I have a number of choices about the actions I can take.

The point is that I can choose to be proactive, or I can be reactive. It's **my CHOICE**. It's not the Reserve Bank that controls my choice.

Although you can't always control a circumstance, you can control your response to it. For instance, some third countries leaders will tell their constituents that the reason they're poverty-stricken is because wealthy western countries use their influence to exploit them and keep them poor. But these same third world leaders were educated in western countries; they drive western cars and wear expense western shoes. Their loved ones study in western academic institutions.

You get my point: they're playing on the pervasive victim mentality in communities like yours to keep their citizens from reaching for more!

"Those who corrupt the public mind are just as evil as those who steal from the public purse." - Adlai E. Stevenson

It's up to you to call them on their nonsense and create the life you want!

In the historically-based Steven Spielberg movie AMISTAD—named after a slave ship that was carrying a cargo of Africans who had been illegally sold into slavery in Cuba in 1839—Cinque, who had been a tribal leader in Africa, leads a mutiny and takes over the ship. They continue to sail, hoping to find help when they land. Sadly, upon reaching the U.S. they're imprisoned and proclaimed runaway slaves. They don't speak a word of English, so it appears they're doomed to die for killing their captors. But an abolitionist attorney takes their case, arguing that they're free citizens of Africa who were illegally captured in Cuba, and not slaves at all.

When the attorney is explaining to Cinque and the other Africans how difficult the argument will be and how almost certain the outcome against them, Cinque responds, "We won't be going there alone. I will call into the past far back to the beginning of time and beg my ancestors to come. At the trial, at the judgment, I will reach back and draw them into me and they must come. For at this moment I am the whole reason they have existed at all."

You are the present living expression, the culmination of a long line of ancestors who were unfettered and determined to survive and thrive. Don't ever let anyone tell you you're anything less than a living, breathing force of nature, capable of accomplishing anything you set your mind, muscle and mettle to.

Don't let your forebears down. Don't let yourself down. Don't squander the gifts you've been given and the gift you are by assuming you don't have what it takes to come out on top.

Of course you do!

CHAPTER TWO

Resign from the 'Ain't It Awful Club'

"Smart doesn't comes from books. Smart comes from making the right decision at the right time in the right place." — Author Unknown

In Step Two, you have a second decision to make. Your choice is between *impotence, helplessness, disdain, and apathy and virility, helpfulness, respecting yourself and others, care and passion.*

Which of these polar opposites do you believe will set you farther along the path to success?

You know the answer.

It's time to submit your resignation from the *Ain't It Awful?* Club and join the *Why Not!* Club. The *Why Not!* Club is based on the familiar quote "Some men see things as they are and ask 'Why?'. I dream things that never were and ask, 'Why Not!"—George Bernard Shaw, Robert F. Kennedy)

Features and Benefits of Both Clubs

The Ain't It Awful? Club asks questions like these:

"Why doesn't somebody do something about the abject poverty we're living in?"

"Why does the government treat us like garbage?

"Who's responsible for letting this go for so long that now our pathetic situation seems like the norm?"

"When are we going to get some relief?"

In sharp contrast, the *Why Not!* Club asks questions like these:

"What one thing can I do today to bring my family, my community and myself a single step closer to self-sufficiency and self-respect?"

"Which government agencies and businesses, here and abroad, can I connect with and influence to help bring an end to the chronic poverty in my community?"

"What can I say or do to model a new reality in my community so that our present challenges appear solvable?"

"What can I do today that will bring a sense of relief and hope to my community?"

The ABC's (features) of *the Ain't It Awful?* Club consist of **A**ccusing, **B**laming, **C**riticizing and **D**istrusting everyone but its own members. The Ain't It Awful? Club *is an exclusive club*: it simply assumes that non-members are oppositional, arrogant, implacable, and dedicated to its subjugation or destruction.

The ABC's (features) of the *Why Not!* Club consist of personal (individual) **A**ccountability, **B**lessing, **C**onsistency and **D**etermination. Instead of being an exclusive club, it embraces inclusivity. It seeks out and encourages cooperation, humility, and agreement, and is dedicated to helping *everyone* survive and thrive.

In a Bygone Era

It should come as no surprise to read that the citizens who made up your country for eons were almost entirely members of the Why Not! Club. Nearly all of them survived quite nicely by encouraging cooperation among members, serving, agreeing on the way forward, and helping every member remain alive, healthy and contributory.

Indeed, this was the case across the globe as individuals and families moved (or were forcibly moved by others) to other areas of the world.

There is zero reason *not* to resurrect the *Why Not!* Club in your community! Its tenets have proven themselves across generations and eons of time. It has only been in the last couple hundred years that things have gone seriously awry in a truly massive way.

So here's your membership application card:

Name:

_____

As a member of the **Why Not!** Club I pledge to personally, unilaterally do something every day that will bring my family, my community, and myself one step closer to recognizing and reaching out to obtain our power, potential and profitability as members of the human race.

I will hold myself accountable and will embrace, help and encourage everyone else who holds himself or herself accountable.

I will not blame, criticize or condemn those who aren't yet onboard under the assumption that when they see what's working for me and others like me, they will become eager to join the club and become enthusiastic, productive members.

Some may never join for various unknown reasons. Club members will not second-guess non-joiners (since everyone is facing unspoken challenges that only professionals can see, diagnose and treat). I will agree to love non-joiners right where they are, honor their decisions, and support them to the best of my abilities.

Starting today—right now—I am dedicating myself to making myself and my community better, stronger, wealthier and happier. My legacy will be, "I cared. I did everything I could to promote peace and prosperity in my community and country."

Signed:

_____

CHAPTER THREE

"If It's to Be, It's Up To Me!"

It is often said that "There is no 'I' in 'team'." True enough. Team work matters.

But the biggest problem, as I see it, is that there is no 's' in 'team'! That is, all too often you'll find no 'steam' in a team! You'll find talk, vision, analysis, and desire, but finding measurable, documentable progress just isn't always possible.

Gather a bunch of people, call them a team, and watch blame the game begin: "I was waiting on _____ to do _____ before I can fulfill my part of the task." "I don't see anyone else doing much to move this along, and I can't do enough on my own to make it all happen." "I don't have the time to invest. Someone with fewer responsibilities needs to do it. But I'm absolutely *committed* to our goal!"

Pretty soon you can find yourself right back in the *Ain't It Awful?* Club!

So here's the deal. *You must hold yourself personally accountable.* You must give yourself daily marching orders and then *commit* to carrying out the tasks you set for yourself—the tasks that, small as each one may be, will get you where you want to go step by step.

Creating a life that lifts you out of poverty is a Do It Yourself project. You can ask for help and you can meet up with other like-minded community members and agree on ways forward. But when it comes to the actual work involved (the sweat equity), that's *your* responsibility. And it will be your joy (eventually) even if it feels like your burden today.

What you build will become your legacy. Your name will be on it. You will be regarded as one of the proactive visionaries who resolutely committed one day to change your world and, in doing so, changed your community and your country.

So don't wait for a team. Don't wait for government. Don't wait for others to figure it out and do their parts to restore dignity and justice to your circumstances.

Do *your* part, every day. When you do, your circumstances *will* change. You'll see progress. You'll feel better about yourself and the future. You'll begin to triumph inwardly because you'll know you're on your way to a better tomorrow.

It won't be easy. You may be tempted to quit more times than you can count. The ultimate triumph may come to your loved ones, heirs, and community some time after you've been shoveled off this mortal coil.

"Let no one be discouraged by the belief there is nothing one person can do against the enormous array of the world's ills. Each of us can work to change a small portion of events. It is from numberless diverse acts of courage and belief that human history is shaped. Each time a man stands up for an ideal, or acts to improve the lot of others, or strikes out against injustice, he sends forth a tiny ripple of hope, and crossing each other from a million different centers of energy and daring those ripples build a current which can sweep down the mightiest walls of oppression and resistance." — Robert F. Kennedy

Martin Luther King Jr. didn't live to enjoy the justice he sought. Nor did Robert Kennedy, Gandhi, or Mother Teresa. But each made a difference that echoes into the 21st century. And each recognized and appreciated the incremental progress that they were able to make during their lifetimes. Certainly the progress must have felt minuscule on most days —but every day brought them just that much closer. Every small advance, every win, fed their hope and prompted their next steps.

It'll be the same for you. Your task is to believe so completely in the goals that you set for yourself that nothing will be able to stand between you and them that you won't find a way over, under, around or through to reach them.

So if you're ready, willing and eager to make a difference that will echo for generations across the globe, *keep reading!* **YOU** *can do this!*

CHAPTER FOUR

Embrace Every Forward-Leaning Opportunity

Here's a sad story from my personal experience. In 2010 and 2011 my U.S. brigade and I were stationed in a Philippines Army camp. Inside the camp was a small free market run by various Filipino vendors. As a procurement logistics guy, I became well acquainted with many of them.

Maria was a quiet, friendly woman who worked for a t-shirt vendor inside the camp. Friday was my weekly re-supply day. I was surprised one Friday to find Maria absent from her usual spot. Figuring she probably wasn't feeling well, I went on my way.

The following Monday Maria was back at the market so I stopped by momentarily to let her know I'd noticed her absence. She told me that her boss was thinking of selling the t-shirt stand and that she would likely lose her job as a result, even though she was the primary caregiver for her ailing father. She was obviously distraught at the way fate seemed to be mocking her dedicated diligence.

I sympathized mightily because I know very well what it's like to be poor and struggling just to make ends meet. Realizing I could do something to help remedy her situation, I offered to help her buy out her boss for $500 (no strings attached) so she could take over the business and control her own destiny.

Two days later, to my utter disbelief and surprise, she turned down my offer! She had allowed the fear of ownership to beat her down. She told me she was afraid to strike out on her own and be her own boss; she said she liked being in the worker bee position—she had been one for twenty years. She felt more comfortable taking orders than giving them.
Perhaps she felt she lacked sufficient business acumen.

But she did ask me if I'd lend or give her the $500 anyway. I said no. Why? Because I knew she would have used it for a temporary fix—as a mere band aid instead of the shot in the arm it was intended to be: the boost that would have given her an actual chance to succeed and control her long-term destiny.

Most people warm themselves at fires they didn't built and drink water from wells they didn't dig. So *it's fine to offer and accept the kind of help that results in forward progress toward the goals you have for yourself, your family and your community. But offering or accepting handouts that serve only a temporary need wastes precious time, money and talent that can be used to correct a situation in its entirety.*

The bottom line: It's how you use what you receive and achieve that matters most.

"Give a man a fish and he'll eat for a day. Teach a man to fish, and he'll eat for a lifetime."

CHAPTER FIVE

Commit to Being a Masterful Steward of Resources

When you take charge of any type of resource—whether the resource is water, wood, money, employees, animals, information, solar, wind, a farm, a vehicle, or anything else — make sure you regard it as the treasure it is.

Don't waste it.

Don't misuse it.

Don't abuse it.

You don't want the economy you're creating to end up operating just like the economies that endlessly-greedy oligarchs have built. (You're in the situation you're presently in because of oligarchs' plots to capitalize on your sweat equity without sufficiently sharing their enormous harvest with you.)

In your new economy, the intrinsic needs and desires of every individual (and creature, if you're raising goats, cattle, chickens, pigs, or other livestock) should be taken into consideration. Your employees should be able to make a decent living (without half killing themselves) and they should share in the monetary rewards of their labors (percentage bonuses based on total net revenues received is one way to ensure this).

In *Fiddler on the Roof*, Tevye says, "When a poor man eats a chicken, one of them is sick." This paraphrase of a Jewish proverb explains, in just a few words, that a single chicken is *usually* far more valuable alive and clucking (because it lays eggs for years—offering nonstop sustenance to its owners—and reproduces to create more egg-producing offspring) than it is dead.

Resources are finite. Some of them feel pain, anguish, and despair. If they do, treat them as well as you'd want to be treated.

Use every resource as if it's the last one of its kind to every extent possible. Doing so will help you honor the intention of this chapter.

CHAPTER SIX

Power Through F.E.A.R.: False Evidence Appearing Real

I want to make one thing perfectly clear—right here, right now: *You Are Enough!*

I want you to overwrite the voices in your head (put there by parental prophecies and current culture) that tell you you're not good enough or ready enough to change your destiny.

What kind of movie is playing in your head right now? Take a close look at it with an objective eye. Is it offering you real hope...or hopelessness?

Outside forces have been messing with your mind. They've polluted it with undisciplined fears, warnings, and other unhelpful notions.

But get this: **You're** a producer and director, too. As a teenager or adult, you're entirely capable of creating a *new* movie in your mind, one that will make you and all of the people you work with and for heroes, overcomers, and winners.

On your tombstone, there will be two dates with a dash separating them, the date you were born and the date you died. Neither date is all that important. It's what you did with the dash in between the two dates (the dash that represents your lifetime) that can make a difference in the world. I don't want you to die with your music still in you.

So in this chapter I want to remind you of one thing and one thing only: **Progress is what matters. Forget perfection. Forget the feeling that you need to be or have anything more than you have right now to make your life, your community and your world a better place.**

Nobody's perfect! We're all doing the best we can, right where we are. And—person by person, day by day, step by step, and breath by breath—everyone is making a difference.

The internal movie that was introduced to you while you were still an infant without the ability to separate fact from fiction has been produced and directed by other people who didn't know you as well as you know yourself. Not even your parents know you the way you know you. They don't know your potential. They don't know your vision. How often have you ever even verbalized your ideal self or your ideal life to anyone?

And why haven't you? Maybe you figure your ideal vision sounds too much like a pipe dream, like pie-in-the-sky, delusional thinking, given your current circumstances.

What is keeping you from going after your goals? Is it fear of failure? Fear of not being good enough, smart enough, or wealthy enough?

Whatever it is, it's probably *an illusion* thrown up by F.E.A.R: False Evidence Appearing Real.

Whenever you imagine the perfect life—whatever that means to you—how many negative feelings also rear their ugly heads?

Let's say you want to become independently wealthy so you never have to work another day in your life unless you want to. If so, do images of the rich young ruler in the Bible stare you down and make you feel greedy for even considering the idea?

Do you worry that you'll be surrounded by needy or greedy people and never enjoy another carefree moment in your life?

Do you worry that your taxes will skyrocket and you don't understand finances well enough to be able to figure out what to save so you can pay them reliably?

Every time you step outside your *comfort zone* (the circumstances you're presently in, no matter how desperate they may be) you run up against F.E.A.R., the invisible wall that screams "Watch out, now! You're entering uncharted waters. There is danger at every turn. You're in over your head. Are you sure you want to do this?"

Risk is always scary. Changing the way you think and what you do always comes with having to unlearn habits and developing new ones that will serve you in the new world you're entering.

Instinctive fear (the fight or flight response) is a good thing when you're up against wild animals, warring populations, and inclement weather. But that's usually *all* it's good for, notifying you of existential (life-threatening) dangers.

The only fears you were born with were the fear of falling and the fear of loud noises. Every other fear you have was learned.

Ask yourself right now: How many of your top ten worst fears have ever been borne out? I'm willing to guess *darned few!* But look how they stopped you. You're not as far along the road to success as you could be because some inane fear held you hostage.

- Many truly amazing, life-changing individuals are held hostage to their status quo anemic incomes by their paralyzing fear of public speaking, or of flying to strange cities, or of talking to strangers.
- Many people are imagining awful outcomes if they defy the expectations that their significant others (parents, peers, community, and/or society) have for them.
- Many people have been conditioned to toe the line, behave just so, and not rock the boat.

Here's the thing. **Fear is manageable.** All you have to do is walk through it to the other side. **Yes, it's scary. That's why it's called fear! But it's False Evidence Appearing Real. Most of what you fear is an illusion.** It won't kill you to walk through it.

In fact, *when* you walk through it, what you'll find on the other side will probably have you grinning ear-to-ear. On the other side of fear you'll find self-respect, opportunity, and successes.

*Your ultimate legacy lies **outside** your comfort zone.*

You're *absolutely* good enough right now to take the next step. Today!

How do I know this? Like me (I too started out dirt poor) *you come from a long line of legacy makers. You're lineage is by way of kings, princes and leaders going back millennia.*

Your story didn't start with you and it won't end with you. So what kind of a legacy do you want to leave?

You're here for a reason: to make a difference.

The question is *what kind of difference* do you want to make?

When you control your head, you control the rest of your body.

Don't just survive: Prevail!

Success is something you'll *attract* as you fully become the person you are.

So become a participant in your own life instead remaining a spectator in someone else's.

Poverty is a choice, not a curse.

You already don't have what you're going after, so you have nothing to lose by going after it—and everything to gain!

So power through! Keep reading!

CHAPTER SEVEN

Become a Leader

"If you want to go fast, go alone. If you want to go farther, go together."

"Seek first to understand, then to be understood." — St Francis of Assisi

At some point, you'll engage with fellow sojourners who buy into your vision for your community and its future prospects. They will want to pitch in and become part of the solution. They will look for direction and marching orders. It is at this point that you'll move from the "If it's to be, it's up to me" paradigm and start choosing the fellows who appear capable of shouldering part of the process.

A true leader ...

- focuses first on other team members' needs before his own
- considers other team members' perspectives
- supports other team members

- appropriately involves team members in the decision-making process
- builds a sense of community

The Result...

- Higher engagement in activities
- More trust among team members
- Stronger relationships
- Increased innovation and transformation

As a leader, you'll focus on other people's *needs*—not on their feelings. This way you'll be able to make the occasional unpopular decision and offer your team or community tough love and negative feedback when it's required.

Leaders are strong, resilient and brave.

You'll give your full attention to others when they're speaking. You'll notice their body language, you won't interrupt, and you'll offer feedback about what they say. You won't judge them on style or approach. You'll always listen for substance and for new things to
learn and consider.

Great leaders talk less and listen more. They're proactive, strategic and intuitive. They understand that they learn more by hearing what others have to say than by regurgitating what they already know and understand.

A leader also realizes "If you can lead yourself, you can lead many."

The best leaders are empathetic; they understand and are aware of the needs, feelings and perceptions of others. They understand team members' challenges and offer help and support whenever doing so will bring mutual goals closer to fruition.

Being a leader isn't rocket science. Indeed, as human beings, we're wired for sociability and attachment to others. Truly engaged people listen carefully to each other, discern each other's struggles and needs from body language and words, and make allowances for human imperfection, missteps and failures. As a leader, you should become a soft place to fall (when falling happens), a safe place to fail (when failure happens) and a serious champion at all times, encouraging your partners onward and upward.

As a leader you'll define the long-term vision and establish the short-term goals that will move every participant in the venture toward the ultimate vision. And although reaching goals will be your over-arching purpose, your day-to-day focus will be on creating meaningful relationships and synergies. To do this, you'll share your ideas and ask team members to share theirs. You'll set the tone and create the positive, pro-active, supportive "can do, will do" culture of your community.

Remember: how people feel colors their perceptions. When your compatriots feel heard, understood and honored by you, they will engage wholeheartedly. To the degree that they feel discounted, misunderstood or ignored, they will disconnect from you and your
vision.

"To know the mind of a man, listen to his words." — Johann Wolfgang von Goethe

"Nobody cares how much you know until they know how much you care." — Theodore Roosevelt

CHAPTER EIGHT

Learn and Employ the Basics of Leadership

According to Brian Tracy, author of How the Best Leaders Lead, there are seven responsibilities of leadership:

- **Set and Achieve Business Goals**
- **Innovate and Market**
- **Solve Problems and Make Decisions**
- **Set Priorities and Focus on Key Tasks**
- **Be a Role Model to Others**
- **Persuade, Inspire, and Motivate Others to Follow You**
- **Perform and Get Results**

Set and Achieve Business Goals embraces every part of strategic and marketing planning, including products, services, people, productivity, promotion, finances, and competitive responses."

Innovate and Market. In Peter Drucker's words, every business is established to "create and keep customers." Innovation (thinking outside the box to stay ahead of the game in your field) and marketing is what creating and keeping customers is all about.

Solve Problems and Make Decisions. Brian Tracy again: "The only obstacles between you and business success are problems, difficulties, hindrances and barriers. Your ability to go over, under, around or through these problems is central to your success."

Set Priorities and Focus on Key Tasks. Time is limited— your options for ways forward and to reach your goal may appear limitless. This is why setting priorities and focusing on key tasks to the exclusion of every other pretty thing (or "scenic route") is crucial to getting where you want to go. Use the limited waking hours you have every day to do something that moves the ball forward toward the goal.

Be a Role Model to Others. The morale of your organization *is* a "trickle down" commodity. Morale must always be established by you. Brian Tracy nails this concept perfectly. He recommends that you ask yourself, "What kind of company would my company be if everyone in it were just like me?" You must conduct yourself as if everyone is watching and mirroring you when it comes to morale, communication and forward motion.

Persuade, Inspire, and Motivate Others to Follow You. The best leaders create additional leaders. So support and serve your team whenever and wherever doing so will advance the cause you're all working for. *Develop leaders and innovators; mere worker bees (people working just to earn money) will never produce the results you need and expect.* The key to achieving sustainable success is earning the trust, respect and confidence of your team.

Perform and Get Results. By being positive, constructive and forward-looking, you will fuel the human engines that are required to perform and get results. Your attitude will determine your altitude. The best leaders lead by example, encouragement and enthusiasm.

According to Brian Tracy, the **Seven Qualities of Leadership** are

- Vision (Transforming dreamers into doers by expressing the ultimate goal and the steps along the way in a captivating, energizing way. Making sure the "why" of your goal is bigger than any obstacle that stands in the way of achieving it)
- Courage (Willing to take the risks necessary to achieve your goals. Every decision is risky. You can't be risk-averse and win anything. Embrace the audacity to seek and put into action the prudent decisions that will carry you to your goal.)
- Integrity (The value that guarantees all other values. In *Winners Never Cheat*, Jon Hunstman declares, "There are no moral shortcuts in the game of business." In any enterprise, the defining difference between commendable success and also-ran vain attempt is character.)
- Humility (Having the self-confidence to recognize the value of others, listen to them carefully and completely without bias, focusing on what's right for the company.)

- Foresight (Recognizing and anticipating future challenges, trends and the actions and abilities of your competition)
- Focus (Deciding what needs to be done, said, and acted upon in every stage of the game, from Day One to popping the cork at the end of your quest and making sure everyone has what he or she needs to get 'er done.)
- Cooperation (Making sure everyone is onboard and rowing together instead of working at odds and slowing down robust forward progress.)

CHAPTER NINE

Become Self-Aware

Becoming familiar with your strengths and weaknesses is more than an inside job. It's all too easy to misjudge other people's reactions and responses when the voices inside your head are yammering away at "what it all might mean".

The best way to discover what other people think about you as their leader is simply to ask them. (If the fear center in your brain is signaling a Yellow Alert as a result of reading this, you *absolutely* need to walk through the fear and do anyway!)

But before you do this, remember to manage your emotions. Acknowledge upfront to yourself that you *don't* know everything you need to know about the way you come across to be able to self-correct. (No one does know how to self-correct and improve until they let down their guard sufficiently to allow and welcome the insights they'll receive.)

Self-awareness gives you tools. By learning what you're good at and what needs to change or improve, you get the opportunity to grow into the kind of leader that others rush to serve, follow, protect, guide, and help.

Becoming self-aware includes…

- Admitting when you don't have an answer
- Owning up to mistakes
- Accepting responsibility for failures and missteps

Consider this. Whether or not you're willing own up to your limitations and imperfections doesn't make them invisible to others. Take my word for it: most of the important ones are readily apparent to anyone who spends much time with you! So it stands to reason that you reveal integrity and encourage transparency whenever you ask for honest feedback on your leadership and communication styles.

By modeling your eagerness and willingness to learn more about yourself from others' perspectives, you telegraph the notion that others should feel free and be comfortable admitting that they, too, make mistakes and that they're welcome to ask for clarification, help and course corrections, too.

A great leader must be like water: adaptable.

You can't change what you won't confront.

A smart person who isn't teachable is a dope.

CHAPTER TEN

Become Persuasive

Which of the following is most likely to convince you to more agreeably take an action that you know you should take, or need to take, but haven't yet taken?

- Authority
- Expertise
- Persuasion/Negotiation

If you're like most people, authority and expertise can come across as unduly authoritarian, coercive, and off-putting, hence the familiar sarcastic quotes, "Who died and left you in charge?" and "An 'expert' (ex-spurt) is a drip under pressure." (Shades of the *Ain't It Awful?* Club mentioned in Chapter 2.)

Leaders use persuasion to encourage action and build consensus. Although expertise can bolster your position (when skillfully introduced), it can't automatically, or unilaterally, cause your team to fall dutifully into line. And authority is truly a double-edged sword when wielded—it can cut both ways—so rolling out your authority is a *really bad idea* most of the time.

Persuasion is a far kinder, gentler, less-adversarial approach to getting the results you want. And as a leader, persuasion is the note you'll be playing on much of the time.

Persuasion is a process of learning and negotiation. Some of your audience may be opposed to decisions that are made by you and others.

Persuasion consists of three phases:
- Discovery
- Preparation
- Dialogue

In the Discovery phase, you'll consider your position from every angle so that all opposing views are well understood. ("Seek first to understand, then to be understood.") To do this, you'll meet with the folks who are sitting in opposition to your plans or decision and hear them out, fully, fairly and respectfully.

In the Preparation phase, you'll anticipate and devise reasonable and respectful responses to opposing views that are as unassailable as possible.

In the Dialogue phase, you'll invite people to discuss all available solutions, debate the merits of each position, and offer honest feedback. You'll test and revise ideas to reflect other people's needs and perspectives. You'll remain open-minded and amenable to learning new perspectives and challenges. Compromise where you can as long as doing so gets you closer to the goal you've set for the project or program.

To remain credible throughout this process, listen carefully to everyone, establish to all concerned that every opinion is honored, and collect information that supports your position.

Because you'll understand your audience so well following the Discovery and Dialogues phases, it should be just a short hop to find common ground and identify the tangible benefits your audience will find compelling and engaging. You may even find that altering your mindset can lead to a compromise that is agreeable to all concerned—a win win situation all the way around.

"Life isn't about how hard you can hit but about how hard you can be hit and keep moving forward." —Les Brown

CHAPTER ELEVEN

BECOME A WARRIOR FOR YOUR CAUSE

"When we recognize our 'warrior self' we can exhibit strength without sacrificing tenderness" – John F. Kennedy

I agree with President Kennedy: The best warriors exhibit tender tendencies.

Most wars, if fact, don't consist of human opponents. They consist of unseen spiritual nemeses whose sole purpose is to lie, cheat and steal people's dreams by convincing us that we don't measure up to the challenges that it will take to overcome the obstacles standing between us and our goals.

An unfettered warrior spirit can overpower and subdue. But a warrior spirit coupled with wisdom and unmerited favor can bless a home, a community, r a nation.

And that brings us to your battle, and to your warrior spirit.

Your battle is a battle for fairness, justice and goodwill. Your battle is to elevate the members of your community, not to subjugate or further marginalize them.

So your heart is engaged and your cause is just. As you draw upon your inner warrior, you'll find clarity, consistency, courage, determination, focus and zeal as constant companions.

Bloom where you're planted. Overrule any tendency you may have to hold back and remain a spectator in your community. Say yes to doing something. Engage. You'll be surprised to discover the number of people who are just waiting to join you to make a difference.

"Courage...is the first quality of a warrior." — Carl von Clausewitz

CHAPTER TWELVE

Visualize the 'Win' That Will Confirm You Met Your Ultimate Goal

"People don't buy on logic. They buy on emotion."

As a leader you're the keeper of the ember that resurrects the formerly- roaring fire. You're the one who fans it into flame on days when it's cold and dreary and very few of your fellow sojourners feel inspired to get up and get going again.

You do this by posing a few questions.

You'll ask things like…

"How will you feel on the day we meet our goal?" and you'll wait for the answers:

- Heroic
- Delighted

- Ecstatic
- Relieved
- Accomplished
- Like a million dollars
- Confirmed
- Cheerful
- Tearful
- Like dancing on the ceiling

"How will your family and community feel on the day we meet our goal?"

- Proud
- Awed
- Fortunate
- Blessed
- Ecstatic
- Delighted
- Cheerful
- Tearful
- Like dancing on the ceiling
- Ready to engage in "whatever comes next"

"If wishes were fishes, how soon do you want to get there?" When you ask this question, you'll probably see grins and hear things like…

- Yesterday!
- Today!
- Tomorrow!
- Soon!

"Since wishes aren't fishes, how fast do you think we'll actually get there if we go after it again, hammer and tong, right after breakfast?

- Next year
- In two years
- In five years
- In ten years
- In twenty-five years
- When my kids are old enough to benefit
- When my grandkids are old enough to benefit

Keeping the vision alive is very much like planting trees that only your children or grandchildren may sit under—but thank God you love them even more than you love yourself!

Some goals take decades of planning to bring to fruition. Yours probably won't. If they do, then you'll need intermediate goals to plan and celebrate on at least a semi-frequent basis or the daily grind can begin to feel thankless and uninspiring.

As a leader you'll be your team's and your community's chief cheerleader and "Dreamer". It will be up to you to keep the vision and the feeling of what success will look like even on days when nothing is going according to plan and your mutual goal seems so far beyond reach—or human stamina—as to make it appear almost unattainable.

Tell the story, again and again, about what breaking down the barriers and succeeding will look like—what it will do for your people, your family, and your future. Ask the people you're with to chime in, to embellish the vision. What will your success taste, feel and smell like? Who will you dance with, sing with, and embrace? What will be a reality that is now only a vision?

Will it be:

- Clean, clear, safe drinking water?
- Solar-powered lights to brighten the night?
- A goat or chicken farm that nourishes and supports hungry families?
- A taxicab company that carries workers to distant work, play and education?

What will your vision-made-real bring to your family and community?

- An honest day's work for a more-than-sufficient honest day's wage!
- Relief!
- A Renewed Sense of Value, Worth and Dignity!

As chief architect of the future you envision, part of your job will be making sure everyone involved remains equally-infected with your enthusiasm and dedication to "getting 'er done". Your foresight and frequent verbalization of the many delights that will accompany the successful outcome of your diligence must never be discounted or under-appreciated.

You'll use your intuition daily to sense the things that are going as planned and the sentiments that are going awry.

You'll remain aware of body language, flagging energies, fears, and other hobgoblins of the mind that signal the need for your attention and intervention.

You'll be looking for the people who don't feel they're winning today, who sense they may be spinning their wheels, and for those who seem to be losing their optimism.

These aren't Ain't It Awful Club folks; they're simply the ones who need you to resurrect the vision and give them a jumpstart.

Or maybe they just need your permission to tend to their own gardens and goals for a spell. Maybe they just need to recover and recoup.

Give them the time. Allow their fountains to fill again. When you do, they'll come back more energetic and committed to "catching up" and finishing their part of the bargain.

Offer to give them any tools you have access to that will make their time away more productive or peaceful. Be their champion so they can be yours when you're at the end of the rope yourself. (Make no mistake: you will be at the end of your rope on some days even if you take pains not to show it. You're human, too!)

Keep the vision of the Final Win so big and so bright that others will ache to play in the glow it casts until the goal is achieved.

CHAPTER THIRTEEN

Commit to 'Growing' Your People

Your team is only as strong as its weakest link. A team member may have embraced the vision and have every ounce of enthusiasm that it will take to reach the goal, but if he lacks the tools he needs to proceed, he'll end up spinning his wheels and slowing your progress. Commit to increasing his competency and your vision will be realized all that much sooner.

Here's your roadmap…

Increase Self-Esteem. When people know, like and trust themselves, there's no stopping them. Make sure that every member of the team knows he's valuable, valued and victorious. (You selected your team keeping these fundamental assets in mind, right?) Always remember that everybody has doubts about their awesomeness—even (and especially) the arrogant, strutting people I'll call peacocks. (I hope there are none of these on your team or on any team you choose. If there are, you may have to disabuse them of their "role" and bring them back to reality.) *Affirm and re-affirm each person's value. Make contact. Stay close.*

Vanquish Fear. Again, a helpful acronym for fear is **F**alse **E**vidence **A**ppearing **R**eal. *(It's noteworthy to remember that newborn babies have only two instinctive fears: the fear of falling and the fear of loud noises. All other fears are acquired.)* In a nutshell, unless you're inside a war zone, about to be involved in a car crash on the freeway, walking unprotected on the Serengeti among hungry predators, or in some other place of potential mortal danger, *most fear is learned and illusory.* Oddly enough, people who are in mortal danger often find that their fear evaporates because they're so focused on making good decisions and achieving a "happy ending" that there's no room left for its potentially-paralyzing influence.

Recognize when members of your team are hesitating for fear of making a mistake or reaching a bad decision. Watch body language, hesitations in speech patterns, the darting of eyes. If you believe something you've said has initiated a fear response, immediately apologize in a lighthearted, compassionate way: "I'm sorry. My tongue got tangled around my eyetooth and I couldn't see what I was saying. Let me re-phrase." *Create an atmosphere of abiding mutual respect and affection so people feel great about who they are and what they're doing, and are unafraid to ask questions or divulge problems.*

Encourage competency. Let your team members know, individually and collectively (transparently) that when (not *if,* when!) they feel they need additional tools, information, data, assistance or discussion to reach their specific identified goals or the next level of competency that will increase their effectiveness so that every hour they spend will increase in value when it comes to reaching the ultimate goal, they shouldn't hesitate to speak up and say so. Let everyone know that no one has all the answers but that, by putting your heads together and making sure each person has what he needs to contribute at his ultimate competency level, you're confident everyone will feel all that much better and reach your ultimate goal all that much sooner.

Respect your people. Treat them like volunteers who have the ability to walk away. (They do, you know, unless you have them under a time-bound legal contract. They may not believe or feel they can walk away, but you should realize that they can!)

Sincere respect is the key to keeping the best people. In fact, the best people won't even stick around if they come to believe that you don't respect them…

Offer development and coaching opportunities. Your team members will need some level of coaching support to learn new skills and reinforce new behaviors. Offer rewards and recognition. Monetary and non-monetary rewards and recognition play a big part in encouraging people to keep on keepin' on. But don't incentivize just the
cumulative results of your team (doing so will drive mediocrity); instead, incentivize and recognize leadership behaviors that make a qualitative difference and any quantitative results that are achieved.

Give team members space to grow into their roles.

Base your recognition on balanced indicators such as individual contribution and team contribution to team performance.

CHAPTER FOURTEEN

Bring Out the Genius in Every Player

"Everybody is a genius. But if you judge a fish by its ability to climb a tree, it will live its whole life believing it is stupid." — Albert Einstein

According to Brian Tracy, the three qualities of genius include

- Focusing exclusively on a single goal, problem or question without getting tired or bored
- Mental flexibility, the ability to consider all the ways of solving a problem or answering a question
- Using a systematic, precise method of reasoning and deduction so a problem can be solved, or a question can be answered, that is reproducible and will work well in similar situations

Brian Tracy says genius-level thinkers avoid *blocking assumptions* (assumptions that may not be true). Tracy identifies five blocking assumptions:

- "Here's a problem. The problem is…" (fill in the blank): it's raining, the market is down, interest rates are higher. *These are facts, not problems, but they tend to stop a lot of people from taking the next step.*

- "I have to solve this problem." Maybe someone else needs to solve the problem, not you.

- "No one else has been able to solve this problem." Perhaps someone *has* faced the same challenge and solved it. Have you looked into the possibility?

- "I have to fix this by (date)." Unnecessary pressure can be a killer. Sometimes problems can be delayed.

- "I have to solve this problem with a single solution." There are myriad ways to solve a problem. Some involve multiple steps. Don't ever be in a hurry to fix something *fast* at the expense of fixing something *better* or even *permanently*.

Be sure your team members are aware of blocking assumptions. This way they can work around them by doing taking the following steps to keep on keepin' on…

Here is Brian Tracy's list (paraphrased) of a systematic problem-solving method:

1. Define the problem clearly in writing. (Example: "We aren't selling enough widgets.")
2. Ask "What else is the problem? (Example: "Our salespeople don't know what to do to increase their success." "Our competitor has a better marketing

campaign." "The big box stores are taking most of our potential customers away."

3. Restate the problem to make it easier to solve. "What do we need to do today to begin to overcome the obstacle?"

4. Determine all of the possible causes of the problem. ("Is our widget equally good or better than our competitor is offering?" "Is there sufficient market for what we're selling?" "Which ad agency or copywriter can make us high-profile so we can compete better?")

5. Determine all the possible solutions to the problem.

6. Make a decision as to which solution to put into action.

7. Assign responsibility for putting the solution into action.

8. Set a deadline and a schedule for intermediate progress reports.

9. Implement the plan.

10. Check to see, later, if the solution was successful. If it wasn't implement Plan B, the solution that you uncovered earlier that seemed almost as likely to succeed as the solution you picked.

If you can share this method of problem-solving with your team of geniuses, you'll be ahead of the game.

CHAPTER FIFTEEN

Build an Effective Team

In *Building Highly Effective Teams, How to Transform Virtual Teams to Cohesive Professional Networks—A Practical Guide*, author Michael Nir identifies the nine *must haves* of a high-performance team:

- Develop clear goals and plans
- Effective communication
- Improve and maintain positive relationships among members
- Clarify roles and responsibilities
- Enhance mutual trust
- Solve problems and make effective decisions
- Value and promote diversity
- Successfully manage conflict
- Provide development opportunities and recognition.

Goals and Plans. People need goals and plans to gain a sense of direction so their efforts can focus laser-like on the results the team is seeking.

Communication. Effective, collaborative communication consists of frequently and consistently being sensitive to each other's needs and challenges, and being transparent and focused on the team's goals.

Relationships. Team members get together frequently enough as friends to hang out and enjoy "down time" with each other. Developing a sense of comradeship and friendliness is crucial. Down time is not wasted time; it allows team members to develop empathy and trust in partners and to self-disclose commonalities, sensibilities and affections for mutual interests: sports, drink, entertainment, family, and more.

Roles and Responsibilities. By breaking down roles and responsibilities, each member of your team will understand his area of responsibility and the deliverables he is expected to bring to the table. Team members also know who the "go to" person is when they need
to collaborate to bring a task to fruition so time isn't wasted wondering who to consult. If you don't define roles and responsibilities, tension, miscommunication, inefficiencies and errors will be the result.

Mutual Trust. This is self-explanatory. Without trust, your team won't be as cohesive, self-disclosing, or mutually-supportive. But trust develops and grows slowly only over time so make sure every activity and decision that you make as a team enhances mutual trust. Nir: "Building trust requires openness, information sharing, honesty, and arguments; trust also enables the free sharing of ideas, which is the basis of the innovation process. Usually…trust is based on intuition and emotions." How *safe* to share and contribute does each team member feel?

Solve Problems, Make Effective Decisions. Review the last chapter for a blueprint on this topic.

Value, Promote Diversity. In a global economy, honoring diversity is an essential. One diversity aspect not often recognized and explored, though, is *generational diversity*. Today (and indeed, for most of recorded history) most communities and teams consist of multiple generations working together for a common cause. By honoring the perspectives and paradigms of other generations, you gain insights you otherwise wouldn't understand or acknowledge.

According to Michael Nir:

Baby Boomers (Born 1946-1964)	Gen X (Born 1964-1980)	Gen Y (Born 1981-2000)
Team Working Style Team spirit/working together/team meetings planned approach	**Team Working Style** Value unique contributions/team meetings planned approach	**Team Working Style** Trust, openness paramount; team meetings only when necessary: little and often
Team Values/Style Common purpose values, must "fit in"	**Team Values/Style** Realize value of diversity but sometimes struggles with it. Enjoys networking aspects of teamwork	**Team Values/Style** Want to know bigger picture/purpose; consider diversity exciting and challenging; status

		unimportant
Preferred Teamwork Medium: Face-to-Face	**Preferred Teamwork Medium:** Face-to-Face but realize virtual is valuable too (although uncomfortable with it)	**Preferred Teamwork Medium** Face-to-Face; virtual; instant messaging
Concerns/Weaknesses Tendency to defer to senior team members	**Concerns/Weaknesses** Reluctant to share knowledge; individualistic; competitive tendencies	**Concerns/ Weaknesses** Can appear "too random" for Boomers and Gen X'ers; may need coaching on project planning, formal feedback mechanisms. Can appear disrespectful to senior team members

Manage Conflict. When conflict is resolved effectively, teams develop stronger mutual respect and renewed faith that they can work successfully through obstacles, challenges and roadblocks. Participants gain insight into successful, mutually-satisfying conflict resolution. Conflict causes individuals to step up their game and learn by listening, engaging, promoting, and compromising where necessary.

Two Theories of Effective Conflict Resolution

Conflict Styles of Kilmann

According to Kenneth Thomas and Ralph Kilmann, there are five basic conflict styles, each with varying degrees of cooperation and assertion.

- **Competitive** (Operate from power, status, rank, expertise, persuasive ability; satisfactory during times of crisis and emergencies, but this style causes bruising and hard feelings in less-dire situations)
- **Collaborative** (Wanting everybody's needs met. Cooperation, acknowledging that everyone is important; good when looking for the best solutions from a lot of viewpoints, when earlier conflicts have surfaced in a group, or when a situation is too important to accept a simple trade-off.)
- **Compromising** (Everyone expected to give up something so everyone can be at least partially satisfied; okay when the cost of a conflict is greater than the cost of losing ground, when equally-matched parties come to a stalemate, and when a deadline is looming.)
- **Accommodating** (Willing to meet others' needs at the expense of one's own. Highly cooperative; good when issues matter more to the other party, when peace trumps winning, or when you believe the other party may reciprocate down the road on another matter.
- **Avoiding** (Conflict evaders take this route. They delegate controversial decisions, accept badly-arrive at decisions, and lean toward not hurting anyone's feelings. Appropriate *only* when victory is impossible, when a controversy is trivial, or when someone else is in a better position to solve the problem.)

Interest-Based Relational (IBR) Approach

This style of conflict resolution respects people's differences of process and opinion while helping them avoid becoming locked into a fixed position.

- Good relationships are Priority #1 (respond calmly to build and maintain mutual respect.)
- Keep people and problems in separate boxes (so valid differences can be debated without harming working relationships)
- Pay attention to interests represented (understand why a person holds the position he or she holds)
- Listen first, speak second ("seek first to understand, then to be understood" so that voicing your opinion will receive the same degree of attention and respect and so you can address the other party's concerns)
- Present the "facts" as you see them: establish and agree on the *objective, observable elements* that will affect the decision
- Explore options together (be open to the possibility that a "third way" might exist that both/all parties can embrace.

Provide development opportunities and recognition.

Review the chapter **Commit to 'Growing' Your People** to refresh your memory on this point.

CHAPTER SIXTEEN
SURROUND YOURSELF WITH POSITIVE PEOPLE

"People are like dirt. They can nourish and help you grow as a person, or they can stunt your growth and make you wilt and die." - **Plato**

You may have noticed a tendency in yourself to "mirror" the energy and emotional output levels of the people you're with. This mammalian instinct to match another's emotional and physiological conditions is innate and crucial in several instances: it helps build fond bonds (reproductive and community value), warn of mutual danger (survival value), and assess and nurture loved ones.

But if you surround yourself with naysayers and energy vampires, your natural tendency to mirror them can sap your energy and make you lethargic, pessimistic and dispirited.

Although you can't *always* choose the people you interact with, when you can, be sure you choose wisely! Your associates' attitudes and energy levels are contagious; they *will* affect your energy levels— and your energy levels will dictate how quickly and how well you'll be able to achieve your goals.

Before committing to a long-term partner to tackle your community endeavor with you, ask yourself a few questions:

- How do I feel when I'm around this person? (Positive, energized, elevated, respected, appreciated? Or minimized, marginalized, anxious, low-energy, disgusted…)
- Has this person not just listened to my vision but responded eagerly and respectfully with helpful ideas and strategies of his own to indicate that he is 100% on board and eager to contribute?
- Does he have the attitude and aptitude we'll need to reliably and responsibly move this endeavor along to completion?

The more honest you are when answering these questions, the better off you'll be.

By recruiting positive, can-do, will do individuals to your cause, you eliminate the potential for negativity and nay saying. You recruit supportive "healers" who are sensitive to mutual needs and will take the time necessary to relieve unintended wounds, encourage cooperation, and make sure everyone stays on the same page and in mutual good graces.

Your goals are challenging enough. Don't make achieving them harder than they need to be. Surround yourself with people who energize you. Steer clear of people who drain you.

CHAPTER SEVENTEEN

Ensure Sufficient (Plentiful) Trusted Communication

It's no secret that high performance teams achieve great results because they develop working synergies that are based on trusted, frequent conversations and communications.

Informal communication creates bonds. Teams that work in close proximity to each other often congregate around water coolers, in break and lunch rooms and in parking lots to exchange ideas and get to know each other better. If you're all centrally located, informal communication is a given, and nearly always a good thing when a team is "on the same page" and engaged in moving the group toward a mutual goal. Encourage and engage in informal communication every chance you get! Doing so can create bonds of trust and mutual affection.

Formal communication creates roadmaps. Regular meetings keep everyone in the loop so the activities of other team members are tracked and so challenges can be addressed and important decisions reached.

Virtual Teams

Of course, teams that are spread across a region, country, or the globe need to pursue other ways to "meet" (informally and formally) using the technology that is available to them via the Internet, smart phones and other avenues (Skype, Google Circles and Hangouts, YouTube, Facebook, email, you name it). Schedule times during the work day
ensure that virtual teams get the informal communications they need to bond as human beings.

Winning Ideas for Informal Meeting Times

During informal meetings, ask for a one-sentence summary from each virtual team member and one favorite personal or work-related quote. Each time, ask one of the team member's—chosen at random—to share something about him- or herself. If the person seems stuck, ask for a brief autobiography or assemble generic questions that any team member would feel comfortable answering.

Weekly or bi-monthly before a scheduled informal meeting, send all team members a video or paper on some aspect of team building or management and ask everyone to weigh in on it during the next get-together to see if there are ways to implement any of the ideas.

Encourage virtual teams to check out whatever "virtual water cooler" you set up for them at least twice a day so they have the opportunity to create and develop fond bonds with their far-flung compatriots.

The bottom line: find reliable ways to connect and have fun on a frequent, informal basis whether your team is in the same location or scattered between Tacoma and Timbuktu. If you want and need high-performance results, ensuring plentiful, trusted interaction is crucial.

CHAPTER EIGHTEEN

Uphold Accountability

Let's assume you've hired the right people. They're motivated, they embrace your vision and goals, they're likeable, reasonable, helpful, and diplomatic self-starters. If this is the case, you're well on your way to meeting your objectives, whatever they are.

But every human being requires accountability partners. It's just too easy to find readily available detours, scenic routes, and excuses for taking a break on the company dime.

Even when your team is virtual, there's a way to ensure accountability. You should have a pretty good idea how long a task should take; time standards for common work tasks have been established. If it appears that a team member is routinely taking significantly longer to deliver than you think they should, it might be time to ask some questions and ask that they install a task tracker on their computer. If they refuse, that's a pretty good sign that you might want to start looking for a replacement. (In some cases, your team member may just need to be moved to a different position if you find him flailing in the position he's currently in and you and he believe he can be a solid contributor in another position. Don't be in a rush to throw out the baby with the bath water.)

If a team member's aptitude is stellar but his attitude begins to plummet, he can bring down the members of your team who interact with him. If you notice the decline in mood and attitude, don't ignore it. Inquire. You may be able to help in some way so his attitude improves. If you see no improvement in his attitude despite your inquiries and attempts to mitigate what's bothering him, it's probably time to start looking for a
replacement with all deliberate haste so you can cut him loose and allow him to seek greener pastures somewhere else.

Remember, high-performance teams are 100% composed of people who want to be there and want to perform gladly at their highest levels of contribution. They shouldn't require much oversight, supervision or accountability checks. Still, the customary accountability check will never put a great team off-stride. In fact, the presence of a robust accountability will help ensure that should a team member begin to struggle with his role or the attitude he carries to it, he will stick out like a sore thumb and his team members will notice. They may even report the change to you before you can spot it. This kind of concerned, *shared leadership* is what keeps most high-performance teams at the top of
their games.

You'll hear more about shared leadership in the next chapter…

CHAPTER NINETEEN

Shared Leadership

Your team will put more effort into plans they help develop than into plans that you develop unilaterally. When team members "co-own" a vision, they're far more likely to operate day-to-day on the understanding that "if it's to be, it's up to me" to do everything in their power to make the vision a reality as soon as possible.

Involve your team in the decision-making process. Identify mutually-satisfying goals and objectives. Watch to make sure everyone is onboard, embraces the objectives and goals, and is equally-driven to achieve the goals you've named and intend to reach. Make sure they know which specific tasks they're in charge of bringing to fruition. Meet formally
and informally to be sure every team member has what he needs to make progress and that he is doing so. When you find someone floundering, marshal your troops and see if, together, you can find a way over, under, around, or through the roadblock he is encountering. If you find he's burning out,

give him some space to recover. If you discern he's lost his passion for the projects he's in charge of, see if another one can re-spark him. If not, look for a replacement.

Your mission, always, is to keep everyone moving toward an end goal that all have identified, want to achieve, and know how to attain.

You shouldn't have to do it alone. You shouldn't have to drag your team using brute strength or will. Instead, harness the cumulative will of everyone who's onboard and keep moving forward incrementally. In a team filled with motivated leaders, there is almost nothing that can stand in the way of accomplishment for very long.

Let your team know they're every bit as much in charge as you are when it comes to the individuals tasks they take on. Give them their rein. Check in often. Help where you can. Get help when you need it.

Inch by inch, life is a cinch. Task by task, power through together. You simply cannot be beaten by outside obstacles or forces as long as you stick together and keep your eyes on the prize: economic stability, community empowerment, and self-respect across the board.

"Nothing is more powerful than an idea whose time has come." —Victor Hugo

CHAPTER TWENTY
CHANGE IS DIFFICULT ... AND DELICIOUS

"A pessimist sees difficulty in every opportunity; an optimist sees opportunity in every difficulty." — Winston Churchill

Nothing lasts forever. You and I will exist as living beings on earth for a limited number of years. So embrace the time you have to make a difference in the here-and-now.

When difficult changes become crucial to moving toward your goals, remember they're temporary, not cosmic neon signs flashing, "Give up! This is too hard! You're just dreaming things could ever get better for you and your community!"

When you get discouraged or fearful, remember to consciously relax your muscles, slow and deepen your breathing, and wait it out. It shouldn't take long to refocus your mind on your reasons for pushing through the obstacles and difficulties that stand between you and the goals you want to achieve.

Remember: the changes you want to bring about are beautiful things. They will restore your community to a time where everyone felt useful and celebrated. They will give your fellows work to do that will elevate their incomes and make life feel completely worthwhile again.

Identify your feelings and re-label them

Fear is the doorway to success. Walk through it.

Anxiety/apprehension/butterflies on your stomach are your body's way of saying, "I'm ready for anything. Bring it on!" (Think of a racehorse at the starting gate—ready to run as soon as the door bursts open.)

Despair is the doorway to hope. Walk through. Begin again. In positive, engaged community activity lays redemption. Hope is contagious. Go out and infect someone else!

The changes you envision will lead to many good things. So embrace whatever it will take to get you where you want to go.

"It is not the strongest of the species that survives, nor the most intelligent, but the one most responsive to change."
~ Charles Darwin

CHAPTER TWENTY-ONE

Apply Tough Love as Needed

It's a foregone conclusion that tough love will be required at points along the way.

The Merriam-Webster dictionary defines tough love this way: "love or concern that is expressed in a strict way especially to make someone behave responsibly."

Responsible parents exhibit tough love when a child is disobedient, wayward or headstrong, when he is behaving (or misbehaving) in a way that is detrimental to himself or others.

In a family situation, tough love is often employed when a teenager begins using or selling illegal drugs. Ouster from the family unit, with an explanation, confirms the message that what he's doing is completely unacceptable and will not be tolerated. Tough love is also underway when a child ends up in jail and his parent refuses to post bail. "If you do the crime, do the time."

Tough love comes from a place of intense affection. Although it's punitive and requires painful correction, it is not characterized by the sentence "I've had enough of you—get out of my sight forever!" Instead, its characteristics are more along the lines of an intervention—there is zero doubt left in the offender's mind that he is considered beyond redemption or re-inclusion in the unit.

Tough love is painful for both (or all) parties. It's nothing anyone enjoys. It severs ties (for a reason, a season, or a lifetime) unless and until the offending party makes an about face and recommits to toeing the line.

When it comes to teams who are committed to an endeavor as purposeful and passionate as repairing your community and giving it sound economic legs to stand on, you would think that tough love should never be necessary. But sometimes it is. Everyone has problems: mental, emotional, or relational. (Only one man has ever walked on water and been without blemish.) So tough love is a foregone conclusion; it *will* be needed along the way. It isn't a matter of *if*; it's a matter of *when*.

Tough love can include *refusing requests, relinquishing all efforts to rescue, refuting another's mistaken beliefs, reprimanding someone who is engaging in harmful behavior, and/or repudiating others (i.e., refusing to have anything to do with them as long as they continue to exhibit the harmful behavior).*

Refuse

You must be willing to refuse the demands and requests of an offending team member.

Relinquish

Relinquish means to give up controlling something or someone. With tough love, you *must* turn complete responsibility over to the offender by relinquishing your desire (or ability) to rescue him from the natural consequences of his actions.

Refute

Allowing the offender to continue to hold a false or harmful belief isn't prudent or caring. You have a responsibility to refute mistaken and harmful beliefs, actions, and attitudes.

Reprimand

Beyond simply refuting mistaken beliefs, you have the responsibility to *reprimand (criticize severely, censure or rebuke)* offenders.

Repudiation

Repudiation trumps reprimand six ways from Sunday. To *repudiate* means to *entirely disown,* to refuse to have anything more to do with an offender. If a tough love intervention doesn't result in the corrective actions required to return a situation to its acceptable baseline, there will come a point when the most prudent decision is to refuse to interact with the person so that (presumably) such extreme repudiation will cause him to stop and reconsider his actions.

It's simply a sad fact: there are times when an individual's behavior is categorically unacceptable, period.

How to deliver tough love

- Right up front, reassure and reiterate to the offender that he is a highly-valued member of the team/community and that only his detrimental decision to act (or not act) in unhelpful/unproductive/risky ways is what is being called into question.
- Leave zero doubt that refusal to respond appropriately (correct a behavior, action or attitude) is a deal-breaker
- If the injury or damage is widespread, involve all parties so everyone knows the offending party has been made aware of the community's decision to give notice that the offense has to stop in order for the consequence not to be meted out
- Reassure the offender that he will be forgiven and welcomed back with open arms as soon as he decides to rejoin the community as a fully contributing member according to the conditions you've outlined

Tough Love Strategy Outline

1. Decide where to hold this difficult conversation
2. Decide who should attend (if anyone) other than the offender
3. Decide the best way to start the conversation. Consider the characteristics and emotional/mental makeup of the person (or team) you'll be meeting with
4. Discern in advance and decide how to handle objections
5. Practice and prepare your presentation, tone of voice, and body language

Practice and Prepare. Before entering a tough love conversation, practice the core content at least five times so you feel comfortable with the topic and can concentrate on the offender's/team's reactions and comments.

Deliver with confidence. Synchronize your words, tone and body language. Use a firm tone of voice. Maintain solid eye contact while speaking. Make sure your facial expressions mirror your message. Maintain an open posture (no arm-crossing or other wrong-headed gestures.)

Follow Up, Reinforce, and Chart Progress. Don't simply move on after a tough love session. Casually check in periodically with the offender or group (the sooner the better, especially the first time) to see if the conversation was fruitful. Reinforce positive actions correct any others (if there are any).

Reminder (although this is an unnecessary reminder to leaders of your caliber): Too much tough love comes across as harsh and hateful, but TLC (Tender Loving Care) isn't everything a real relationship requires, either. A finely-tuned balance of the two is productive, helpful and healthy.

Remember this, too: Research indicates that you should offer at least five times as much praise and TLC as tough love. So remember to praise (to the moon and back) positive, pro-active actions and behaviors; don't make the mistakes of just taking them for granted. This way when you have to get tough, there will so much goodwill in everyone's emotional bank account that the occasional withdrawal will seem both palatable and acceptable. When individuals receive mostly-positive interactions with you, they're far more willing to accept and respect the tough love you occasionally have to mete out.

TLC can include giving tangible small appreciated gifts and gestures, spending quality time, talking and listening in affirming ways, doing caring tasks, and bestowing friendly slaps on the back and "atta boys" in abundance. Make the workplace as much fun as you can and you're 90% there.

CHAPTER **TWENTY-TWO**
BECOME A CHANGE AGENT

"If you don't create the change you want to see in yourself and your community, nothing <u>will</u> change—except for the worst." - **Dr. Matondo Wawa**

Inertia—standing or sitting in one place, wishing and hoping only—is a recipe for stagnation, not for transformation.

As a visionary and leader, you will be recruiting and encouraging others to join your cause to help you make your vision for your community happen. There's just one challenge to overcome: getting the people you want to recruit believing that their actions can truly change the future in ways that will elevate them and their loved ones.

Speaking from my own experience, until I got a big wake-up call from my mother—a call that re-animated my enthusiasm for the going after the best that life has to offer, I was a fence-sitter, watching my brother excel and get all the applause and kudos. I was sullen, jealous, and far too angry for my own good—or anyone else's—and I portrayed that to the world.

After my wake-up call, I realized that what had been stopping me was me—not my circumstances, not my surroundings, nor anything else. What needed to change was ME! As soon as I embraced this fact, I became unstoppable. Since that day, I've lived in five countries, changed schools five times, and have dived into five different satisfying careers. Life is good and always getting better! So what's not to love about embracing and promoting change and the possibilities that it can reveal and deliver to your life and community?

To be sure, moving from country to country impacted me. In committing to embracing change, I became more flexible and open-minded. Today I understand and embrace cultural differences and revel in the diversity of peoples that our planet offers.

Each of my career shifts added knowledge and new experiences. I learned how to resolve conflicts and work successfully with the crucial difficult people that moving forward requires occasionally.

I developed self-confidence.

All of these positive changes felt so good that I developed a passion for change. Instead of listening to the fearful clamoring that went on inside my brain, warning me that I was stepping outside my comfort zone, I developed a paternal attitude toward it. I'd advise myself "Sure, this is all new and feels awkward and scary. I'm moving forward anyway."

Make no mistake: ***even if you resist or avoid change, it's going to happen***. You can be a reactor—the person ***affected*** *by* the change—or you can be a responder—the person *creating* it. Needless to say, when you're in charge of the change, the outcome is always going to be better than if you resign yourself to whatever is evolving from the actions or inactions of others. And adapting to changes you love will always be far easier than adapting to changes you loathe. Convince others in your community of this wisdom, and you'll make progress.

So here are ten powerful benefits of change and how to convince the fence-sitters in your community to embrace it.

1. Although difficult at first (overcoming inertia and fear is always tough), making a positive change eventually results in a pleasant victory, making the next necessary change toward a positive outcome more palatable and easier to commit to.

2. Proactive change results in accelerated personal growth. You evolve into the person that your undamaged essence knows you to be.

3. You become less rigid and more flexible. Embracing changes allows you to adapt to new situations, environments and people, all of which open up new opportunities for learning and progress toward whatever it is you're going after. You don't panic when something shifts unexpectedly; you adjust your sails.

4. Improvements start showing up. Finances, jobs, partners, accommodations. Without embracing change, nothing can improve.

5. Your values will either change or become more solidified as you reevaluate your beliefs and begin to see things from different (perhaps

formerly alien) perspectives.

6. Small incremental changes can grow into massive, community-altering changes in the same way a snowball, created between two hands, can accumulate snow and become huge when rolled along snow-covered ground.

7. Good changes may require periods of disconcerting, painful changes. When an existing road is being repaired, sections of old one get torn up. As you make changes, you'll develop the wisdom to know—and strength to say—"This thing has to go before the construction can begin."

8. Change triggers progress. Step-by-step, day-by-day, things will move along in the direction of your goals.

9. Every change will offer up a new opportunity, or opportunities. Additional choices will appear. If they'll contribute to reaching your goal, embrace them. If they offer something that feels even more compelling than the road you're on, you'll need to make a choice to stick with the program or embrace and pursue the new one. Perhaps you can do both. Either way, you'll have additional opportunities to achieve more

10. Your same'ol' same'ol' routine life will be no more. You'll become eager to jump out of bed every morning to engage and encounter whatever the next step is along the way.

"The price of doing the same old thing is far higher than the price of change." ~ **Bill Clinton**

CHAPTER TWENTY-THREE

MAKE IT DO-ABLE: TAKE IT ONE DAY AT A TIME

"The best thing about the future is that it comes one day at a time." – Abraham Lincoln

When envisioning your ideal future, it's always best to imagine its sights, sounds, smells and delights, to put yourself there in your imagination so fully that the thought of failing to accomplish it gives you real pain.

The only problem with doing it this way is that, once you've "visited" the future that doesn't yet exist you may feel inadequate or overwhelmed when it comes to achieving it. That's why it's important to remember that the future arrives incrementally across time. You can't pole vault your way there.

Every great endeavor takes time, tools and the right temperament. The Great Wall of China and the great pyramids took many decades to build Even with 20th century equipment the Grand Coulee Dam in Washington State took eight years to build; the Aswan Dam in Egypt took eleven years. What can seem an "impossible dream"" becomes entirely possible when it's broken down into actionable steps and divided up into tasks for your teams.

What you can do immediately after envisioning your future is develop an actionable blueprint that will ensure *measurable progress* from day to day.

If you're working with a team or a crew, you know their skills and abilities. You know where they excel and where their weaknesses lie. You know which people, processes and systems you'll need to bridge the chasm that exists between where you are now and where you're determined to end up.

By taking every possible action that presents itself—every positive step that leads you in the direction of your intended future—you will bolster your desire to arrive. Nothing will stop you. You will be on your way every day, rain or shine.

Your community's present predicament will be alleviated as you progress and ultimately eliminated when you arrive. Keep your eyes on the prize. Jump start your journey starting tomorrow. Dream so big today that you'll dedicate your best efforts to your community tomorrow.

CHAPTER TWENTY-FOUR

SHOW UP TODAY TO LEAD THE WAY TO THE FUTURE YOU WANT

"Follow your bliss and the Universe will open doors where there were only walls." – Joseph Campbell

Every life is lived in the **here and now**. Yesterday's actions are in the past, as are the things you did five seconds ago. Tomorrows aren't reachable yet. If this doesn't settle you into a calmer perspective, nothing will!

If you do what you need to do right now (whatever it is that will bring you a step closer to your goal), **tomorrow will take care of itself**. Just develop the skills and relationships you need and do the work, and the future you envision becomes a real possibility instead of a pipe dream.

Engage wholeheartedly. Work ardently. Listen carefully. Adjust accordingly. Every day. Day after day. "Enjoy your achievements as well as your plans." (Desiderata)

You need not completely understand everything that's happening. Harmonize with your team and make steady progress; that's all that's required.

Your journey can become as satisfying as your arrival as long as you don't rush things. Manage your emotions so they engage and encourage your team at every turn, energized by the work they perform.

Helping your team remain mindful (fully present in the here and now and in a calm, relaxed frame of mind) will bolster their effectiveness and ensure that they'll want to re-engage wholeheartedly tomorrow and for all the days afterward until you cross the finish line together at journey's end.

As a community leader, you'll set the pace, establish the culture, and exalt the participants. Your job is to encourage and inspire, promote a positive working environment, lead by example, and make sure everyone is following the blueprint. Be curious and willing to engage. Ask for what you want or need and provide what your team wants or needs. When you show up, the Universe responds by providing what you need to succeed.

"To the mind that is still, the whole Universe surrenders." – Lao Tzu

"Live in the present and make it so beautiful it will be worth remembering." – Ida Scott Taylor

CHAPTER TWENTY-FIVE

RELEASE REGRET

"I made decisions that I regret, and I took them as learning experiences. I'm human, not perfect, like anybody else." – Queen Latifah

"The regret of my life is that I have not said 'I love you' often enough." – Yoko Ono

"It is better to look ahead and prepare, than to look back and regret." – Jackie Joyner-Kersey

"We should regret our mistakes and learn from them, but never carry them forward into the future with us." – Lucy Maud Montgomery

Everyone has experienced regrets. The wisest among us release them so our emotions and energy levels are no longer held hostage by them.

Maya Angelou is famous for saying, "When we know better, we do better."

Yesterday's missteps, regrettable actions and inactions are behind you if you'll agree to leave them there. You can't un-do what you did, or failed to do. You can only learn from the pain or injury it caused you or another and move on.

If you know, to a dead certainty, that you'll never do it again (the consequences were too dire!) you have learned what you needed to learn, and you need to move forward. You're wiser and better off than you were. Focus on what's possible now.

Nobody gets through life lily white. Everybody has messed up. Be a good counselor to yourself. Dust yourself off, square your shoulders, and forgive yourself in the same way a devoted parent would.

Until you do, you'll be working at a distinct disadvantage. You need to love yourself to tackle life again with all you have to give. Regret will slow you down, cripple your forward motion, and convince you that you don't deserve the future you're going after.

It's all a lie. You have too much to offer to let past mistakes and regrets determine your fate.

CHAPTER TWENTY-SIX
IF YOU DECIDE TO DO NOTHING AFTER
READING THIS GUIDE, READ THIS!

"The only thing necessary for the triumph of evil is for good men to do nothing." – Edmund Burke

Although I've poured my blood, sweat and tears into this effort, a guidebook can only be as good as the person who's reading it.

So if *all you do* after reading this is put it back on the shelf—that is, if you fail to take action—I can guarantee you that something *is* going to happen to your community and to yourself that you helped cause. It probably just won't be the change that *you* and your loved ones want.

And wouldn't that be a shame? You know it would.

Here's the deal. If you've stayed with me this long, I *know* you have what it takes to transform yourself and your community into something substantially superior to what you have right now.

Tomorrow is coming whether you take action today or not.

If you want it to be different in a good way, you've got to do something because you've just read a resource that shows you the way. You know more than you did. Others don't have the same advantage. You have to lead, follow or get out of the way.

Please don't bail. Remember why you started. Remember why you read this. You know there's more to life and living than what your community and you ate experiencing today.

The thoughts you think, the words you speak, the actions you take "cues" others to take action. You are *already* impacting the world. By deciding to sit on the sidelines, you're impacting the sidelines—encouraging other sideline sitters to "sit this one out" and remain a spectator to an unfolding future that you will have to live in.

So there is really no excuse to linger and languish. There is every reason to engage and energize those around you so they'll want to engage, too. Whatever is speaking to your heart—whatever led you to read this book—*needs you to engage and win!*

In Conclusion

My mother told me something immensely powerful when I was a teenager. My older brother was excelling in every area of life—and my nose was a little out of joint because of it. When I bellyached to my mom that he seemed to be getting all the breaks, she responded calmly and with love, "Your brother is applying himself. You're just as bright, just as talented, and just as capable. But you don't apply yourself. You just coast."

I realized she was right. That's the day I decided to turn my life around and go for the gold. And I have never looked back—except in gratitude for the gift my mother gave me that day when she told me the painful truth.

This guide offers you a roadmap to a future that is far better than the one you see ahead of you right now. This has been the plan all along: to give you hope and a future worth working for.

There will be times along the way when you'll want to quit. When this happens, remember why you started! Remember that you're standing on the shoulders—on the blood, sweat and tears—of your ancestors. You were their hope and you are their present legacy to the world.

If what you want to achieve was easy, you and everyone else would already have it. You aren't late; you're right on time. God planted you in the right place at the right time so you can make perfect use your skills and talents to create a better outcome than the one that appears to looms before you now like a dark, gray cloud.

When you have a bad day, remember that a day only lasts 24 hours; then you get a new one.

Without failure and setbacks there can be no success. Work with purpose and persistence and you'll get there.

You have a mission. You have a passion. You have a legacy to leave. What's it going to be?

You are unique in the world. There is no one else exactly like you. The world is aching for the help, wisdom and blessings you can bring to it.

Don't wait. There will never be the 'perfect time' to begin… so begin right now because *right now* is all you have to make tomorrow better than today is. And you can do it.

I believe in you. Power through!

REFERENCES

Chapter One

* Isaac Prilleltensky and Lev Gonick (1996). Polities change, oppression remains: On the psychology and politics of oppression. Political Psychology, 17, 127.
* Janet Lehman: "It's Not Fair!" How to Stop Victim Mentality and Thinking in Kids and Teens.
http://www.empoweringparents.com/How-to-Stop-Victim-Mentality-Thinking-Kids.php
* Henrick Edberg: How to Break Out of a Victim Mentality: 7 Powerful Tips.
http://www.positivityblog.com/index.php/2009/10/09/how-to-break-out-of-a-victim-mentality-7-powerful-tips/
* Thomas J. Nevitt: The Victim Mentality.
http://aaph.org/node/214

Chapter Two

* John G. Miller: QBQ: The Question Behind the Question (2001, 2012). What to Really Ask Yourself to Eliminate Blame, Victim Thinking, Complaining and Procrastination.
http://amzn.to/1Gp7wpE

Chapters Eight and Fourteen

* Brian Tracy, How the Best Leaders Lead (2010).
http://amzn.to/1OhTv3B

Chapters Fifteen and Seventeen

* Michael Nir, Building Highly Effective Teams, How to Transform Virtual Teams to Cohesive Professional Networks—A Practical Guide. http://amzn.to/1V8oUdh

Chapter Twenty-One

*Marty Seitz, Wellness Matters: When 'tender' love is insufficient, give 'tough' love a chance to work
http://www.kyforward.com/our-health/2013/02/21/wellness-matters-when-tender-love-is-insufficient-givetough-love-a-chance-to-work/
*Doug Van Dyke, Leadership Simplified,
http://www.leadershipsimplified.com/e-learning/newsletters/howto-deliver-difficult-conversations

About the Author

Dr. Matondo Wawa served in the United States Army for 25 years, receiving numerous awards:

Bronze Star
Meritorious Service Medal
Joint Service Commendation Medal
Army Commendation Medal
Army Achievement Medal
Armed Forces Expeditionary Medal
Liberation of Kuwait
Operation Iraq Freedom
Army Service Medal

Dr. Wawa received his Doctor of Management, Leadership Management from Phoenix University in 2011.

In 2006 he received his Masters of Science in International Management and Healthcare from Troy University.

In 2000 he was awarded a Bachelor of Arts in Film from the University of Las Vegas.

Dr. Wawa is a U.S. citizen and a native of Congo. Dr. Wawa is Founder/CEO of Purpose Investment Group and Purpose International Inc., social enterprise companies devoted to alleviating poverty in chronically-poor communities.

Visit his websites at www.purposeinvestgroup.com and www.purposei.com.

About the Purpose Investment Group

PURPOSE INVESTMENT GROUP exists to deliver the specific resources you'll need to establish a sustainable, thriving small business. You'll supply the heart, integrity and sweat equity that is required to keep any reputable business in operation long-term.

Are you ready to embrace the success that awaits your unique skills, talents and commitment? If you are, team up with Purpose Investment Group today.

Which of the following enterprises intrigue you?
Let us hear from you!

- Solar energy
- Clean water
- Agro-culture
- Transportation Fleet
- Medical product assistance
- Micro-finance
- Retail

To engage further, email **purpose_01@yahoo.com.**